I have a talent for writing
My mom has a talent for typing

"Thanks (Rivé) for sharing your wise insights with us less knowing beings."
   —Dr. Erik Tysklind, Veterinarian

"Rivé has lots to say. She leaves you wanting more."
   —Susan Smith, owner City Dog Grocery Store and columnist for the *Broad Ripple Gazette*.

Thoughts, Oughts, Naughts:

Poems from the Heart of a Very Special Dog

by Rivé Wood as told to

Patricia Walworth Wood

Illustrated by Laura Hildreth

iUniverse, Inc.
Bloomington

Thoughts, Oughts, Naughts:
Poems from the Heart of a Very Special Dog

iUniverse books may be ordered through booksellers or by contacting:

iUniverse
1663 Liberty Drive
Bloomington, IN 47403
www.iuniverse.com
1-800-Authors (1-800-288-4677)

Because of the dynamic nature of the Internet, any web addresses or links contained in this book may have changed since publication and may no longer be valid. The views expressed in this work are solely those of the author and do not necessarily reflect the views of the publisher, and the publisher hereby disclaims any responsibility for them.

Any people depicted in stock imagery provided by Thinkstock are models, and such images are being used for illustrative purposes only.

Certain stock imagery © Thinkstock.

ISBN: 978-1-4620-1570-2 (sc)
ISBN: 978-1-4620-1571-9 (e)

Printed in the United States of America

iUniverse rev. date: 07/27/2011

Books by Patricia Walworth Wood

Just Being Me: The Path of a Poet

The Rivers Flow: The Kanawha and Ohio Valleys, 1930–1960

In Memory of Rivé
7/11/97-6/22/11

Acknowledgments

I wish to thank my husband; without him, I could do no writing. He puts up with a lot, such as my late nights and getting up late in the mornings or being late getting meals on.

There would be no Rivé without my brother and my sister-in-law. Rivé was a gift from them.

The guidance from the iUniverse publishing staff was invaluable.

And without Ron Berry's able technical assistance, I couldn't have gotten the manuscript into the proper format for publishing.

Phyllis Beatty gave me support in more ways than one, including reading the manuscript before I sent it in.

I also want to thank Myrla Wagner for reading the manuscript and for her support.

My creative writing group, a study group of the American Association of University Women, heard many of the poems and critiqued them for me.

Thank you, one and all.

Many true stories have a disclaimer that any errors are the author's, not those of the true people who are involved. In this case, the author wants you to know it is the typist's fault, not the author's.

Also I, as the typist, stress a disclaimer about Rivé's poetry. I want you to know that the opinions expressed here are solely those of the author, not this typist.

Contents

Introduction

A New River

I have a river
In my life once again,
A river that runs
Faster than the wind
On a blustery day,
Dashing without care
And wearing a coat
Of soft white hair.
I am referring
To my bichon frise,
Whose name is *River*
But pronounced *Ri-vay*.

At the time Rivé became a part of our family, I had just started writing a book, *The Rivers Flow: The Kanawha and Ohio Valleys, 1930–1960.* This book covers what it was like to grow up in that time and area as it was experienced by myself and others. I wanted to give her a name relevant to my book. Kanawha, Nawha, Valley, or Mountains didn't sound right, so I created River (Ri-vâ). I soon eliminated writing the *r* at the end of the word because it was a silent *r*, but I continued with the same pronunciation.

The idea for Rivé to write poetry came from Rita Mae Brown's cat, Sneaky Pie, helping her write her mystery books. After all, if a cat can help write a mystery book, then a dog can write poetry and create a book.

Welcome to Rivé's world.

Part I

In the Beginning

I Can Too Write

Some of you are skeptics;
Don't deny it, 'cause I know.
I see your faces,
I hear you laugh, and so

I'll tell you how
I'm able to write;
I compose in my head
And then gently bite

Mom's clothes to pull
Her to the keys.
I climb up and poke
Her fingers with ease.

I poke them in order,
Nudging each one down,
Which is how I've become
A poet of renown!

A Good Cause

These verses have been written
for a very good cause:
that very good cause
is, of course, me.

But not just for me,
but for my brethren and *sistren*,
so you will know
all in our hearts because

I can write well,
since I have the genes,
and my mom to type
as she listens to me.

So, take heed,
read well, and understand
what we four-leggers
think, know, and see.

Author's Note
If the plural of *brother* is *brothers* or *brethren*, it surely follows that
the plural of *sister* is *sisters* or *sistren*.

The Wind and I

I like the wind
to hit my face
and carry to me,
if only a trace,
every scent
in the air,
while the wind
combs my hair.

5

Part II

Thoughts about My Mom and Me

Messy Desk
(Neat Mom)

My mom's desk is so messy;
I don't see how she can type
My poems, but she does,
So I can't gripe.

All I have to do
Is to just be me
And allow to flow
My creativity.

My Mom Is …

I've got a secret
about my mom,
but you've got to promise
not to tell her foes;

I don't want to
have to take an oath
on the witness stand—
you know how that goes.

Anyway, back to Mom's
strange behavior.
We have this white, wet,
cold stuff all around.

I don't want to lie in it,
but tonight, crazy Mom
(this is the truth)
lay in it, on the ground.

While there, she moved
her arms and legs;
if she wanted to get warm,
I'd think she'd go in.

But no, she lay there,
moving them up and down;
what I want to know is,
has she gone 'round the bend?

(Mom says, "Twelve years later, I'm still making
snow angels!")

Aromas

My mom
creates,
in the kitchen,
wonderful smells,
but does she share?
No.
She just always tells me,
"Get down,"
and does so
wearing a frown.

You agree,
don't you,
that it's not fair
for her to allow
tantalizing aromas
to fill the air
and then keep
the sources
for herself,
Daddy, and Grandma,
when all I want
is a lick
or a gnaw?

No Fair

My mom is fat;
I'm getting there too,
but without eating
what Mom gets to.

She fills up her tummy
with lots of sweets,
while I only chew
on little dog treats.

Each time my grandma
sneaks me a bite
of her chocolate candy
or any sweets in sight,

Mom yells, "No."
That's not fair.
My grandma is nice;
she knows how to share.

When my mom bakes,
it's for Dad and herself,
while my food always
comes dry from the shelf.

Mom isn't nice;
she doesn't share,
which isn't fair.
It's *just not fair.*

The Rivé Diet

Forget the food,
But eat the treats;
Drink some water,
And then life is neat.

Formulated by me after a weight gain

On Track

If it wasn't for me,
Mom wouldn't stay on track.
She wouldn't get to bed,
and that's a fact.

And she needs me to say,
"Mom, it's now time
for you to write."
I absolutely shine
in my ability to guide
her through the day.
I know what's next
to come her way.

All she needs do
is to listen to me.
I know her schedule:
one, two, three.

Where Are You?

Mommy, Mommy, where are you?
Why didn't you come home last night?
For a very long time,
you've been out of sight.

I hope you haven't
left Dad and me,
but Dad doesn't seem worried,
so I guess I needn't be.

I wish Dad knew
the language for my ears;
maybe then, if he did,
I'd have no fears.

But Dad doesn't get it,
about words I know;
he doesn't speak
the way Mom does, so

I'll wait by the door
again tonight
and hope she will soon
be in my sight.

A Growl Away

I took my mom
for a walk last night.
It was a lovely time
beneath the starlight,
but then I looked
across the street
and saw two dogs,
big and sleek.

They made me nervous
so I gave them a scowl,
tugged at the leash,
and started to growl,
but my mom said,
"Stop that, no,
sit, stop, sit,"
and she wouldn't let me go.

I just wanted to give
those dogs a scare;
with my growl,
they wouldn't dare
come after Mom
or stomp on me.
My growl is fierce;
they'll leave us be.

On Kissing

Mom told me today
My verse has been missed.
Hearing that news
Is like being kissed,

Which reminds me to say
Humans don't know
The very best way
To let affection show.

Stop and watch me;
You'll see my tongue go,
Licking, kissing you
From head to toe.

Thus I'm kissing you,
Cleaning you too,
My best way to show
I love you true.

This was written in response to Marjorie Snodgrass's question: "Has Rivé written any new poems?"

©L.HILDRETH

Time for My Desires

I don't know why Mom
won't do what I want at night
when I am sweet and
do what she considers right
all the rest of the time,
such as letting her write,
or talk on the phone,
or stay up till midnight.

I take care of the house
when she is away,
which seems to be
most of every day.

I let her know
if someone's at the door,
and I love her lots, though
she can be a bore.

So why can't she learn,
since she is bright,
to let me out
in the middle of the night?

Sometimes, I have to
show her what is right,
though it means peeing
in her room at night
(on the newspapers, of course).

Top Dog

Mom,
when are you going to get it?

I've taken care of you
for six years,
but your understanding
has been in arrears.

Take today.
You gave me a ride in the car
and then let me out
at the beginning of the trail
and said,
"*No*,
we're not taking the trail today."

Where did you get this "we" stuff?
I had already decided
we were to walk;
it was not your choice.

You should know by now
who the top dog is.
I am, but
I'll share.
When it suits my mood,
I'll go along with you,
but hey, that's my decision,
not yours.

I think it's time
you learned all of this.
It would make our lives
go smoother.

Think about it, Mom.
Now do you know
who is top dog?

Mom's note: For a year, we went to McDonald's three days a week, but before I'd go inside, we would walk the hiking/biking/skating trail that passed by there. I didn't want to walk that day, but when I let Rivé out of the car to tie her to an outside table while I got my food, Rivé dragged me to the trail. She's strong!

My Way

My mom wants me
To go her way,
But I say *no*,
And I hold sway.

I am strong,
Stronger than the wind.
Thus I am always
Going to win.

Give it up, Mom;
I know what is best
For me and for you,
So give it a rest.

The Smells

I heard my mom say,
"She smells like a dog."
I certainly hope so;
I'm no yucky hog.

No two-leggers ever
Smell like a rose;
In fact, some of them make
Me wrinkle my nose.

But Mom's smell,
Well, it's Mom's smell,
And I love her,
So her smell is swell.

Part III

The Yucky Stuff, Including Naughts

I'm Sick

Neither my mom
nor my doctor knows
why I'm sick from
my head to my toes.
I don't want to talk
to those who walk by.
And I don't care
if anyone says hi.
Going up and down stairs
is very, very hard,
and I refuse to go
very far from my yard.
Please, new doctor,
find out what is wrong.
All I want is to be happy
and bark a cheerful song.

Hospital Stay

Yuck!
I was very happy
when you, Mom, came to
spend some time
with me.
But I couldn't
let you leave
without marking you
with my pee
so that all
will know
you belong to
me!

New Doc

Mom has taken me
to a new doctor again.
I hope this one
will heal my skin.
I'd like to be beautiful
inside and out.
It doesn't matter to Mom;
she loves me, no doubt.
She doesn't care
if I'm no longer called cute,
not with my skin:
the sores are acute.
Well, new doc,
what do you know?
Can I look better?
Will the bad spots go?
Mom, Mom,
please, spend the money;
please, remember
I am your honey.

A Job

Me? A job?
Mom told the vet,
"She needs to get a job."
I have a job.
Who takes care of the house
When she and Dad are gone?
Who is on duty
At all times,
Caring for them at home?
I take care of them on trips,
And I take care of the car
When they go and stuff their faces.
Wake up, Mom;
Pay attention.
I have one job,
And that is plenty.
And I do it out of love,
So can't you do the same?
(Pay the vet, Mom.)

And now, writing and selling my book is my job too. Spread the word, please.

I'm Well

I didn't think
I'd be well again.
That yucky feeling
Would never end.

Day after day,
I couldn't talk or eat.
I didn't have the energy
To lick Mom's feet.
And then Dr. T.
Tried something new.
I was so happy
I didn't know what to do.
My mom and dad
Said, "Hooray,"
And so did others.
I'm happy today.

©L. HILDRETH

(These next three poems are rated CG: Child Guidance.)

Payback Time

Mom left me behind,
But what did I care?
Now that she's home,
She'll quickly be aware
That I have accidents
Here and there.
From now on,
She best beware
And leave me home
Only if she dares.

Oh Poop, I'm Sorry

Mom, Mom,
Why are you so mad?
Why aren't you happy?
Why aren't you glad
That I'm not a bother
When you are so busy?
Caring for Grandma
Keeps you in a tizzy.

And I couldn't wait.
All I did
Was just a little poop.
It wasn't much;
You didn't need a scoop.

Mom, I'm sorry
I made you mad.
I was trying to help
And make you glad.

Messed-Up Carpet

Mom invited two men in:
"Carpet cleaners," she said.
I say nuisances who
should have stayed in bed.
Their noisy machine
messed up my place,
erasing every trace
that I live here.
This is my land,
so I took matters in hand.
I had to act promptly,
quicker than I bark,
going in many places
to leave my mark.
In this manner,
I took back my space
so that everyone who enters
knows they're in my place.

Part IV

My Thoughts, Mom's Oughts

The Sweatshirt

My mom wears a sweatshirt
That makes no sense at all.
It shows a bichon
On a long phone call.
But at our house, it's Mom
With the phone on her ear.
She seems to talk forever,
And this is what I hear:
"Yakity, yakity
Yakity yak,"
And on and on
For she has that knack,
According to Dad,
For being a *drone*
(Whatever that means)
Since she is always on the phone.
So whenever he comes home
And speaks to her—"Dear,
I want to talk to you"—
The phone is against her ear.

The sweatshirt shows a bichon frise on the phone and this verse:

> The Bichons came into their own
> Long after their days on the throne.
> They would much rather talk
> Than go out for a walk.
> Now you can't get them off of the phone!

©L·HILDRETH

Talking

I heard my mom
tell her friend
(Mom does have one or two)
about her dream
where I talked,
but then that's always true.
I speak to Mom
all the time,
not just in her dreams,
no matter what
anyone thinks,
no matter what it seems.
How else does Mom
ever know
just what I'd have her say
when she types my verse
(which she does well)
as she does today?
Oh, my silly mom:
I do love her so,
but I fear sometimes
she doesn't know
what she knows,
or else doesn't let it show.

Seeing Red

Everywhere I look,
I see red.
I see it when my mom
Goes to bed.

I see it on our walks;
My lead, you see, is red,
As is my mom's cane
And the hat on her head.
Look at Mom's new clothes:
RED.

The Squirrel and I

Come down, little squirrel;
come down and play;
I'm all alone—
at least, I am today.

And you have a nut,
which I'd like to see;
it's fun to play with—
at least, it is for me.

You have so many friends
to chase around a tree;
I'd like to run too,
to chase and be free.

Please, give me a chance.
I'm just a youth;
I won't hurt you,
and that's the truth.

Please, brown squirrel,
please, come down to play;
we'll have much fun
on this gray March day.

Go, Colts, Go

"Go, Colts, go,"
My mom yells at the TV.
Go where?
If she says that to me,
She wants me
To go outside and pee.
Would those men
Dare do that on TV?
I don't think so,
But well, we'll see.

Silly Things My Mom Says

In the doghouse,

My dogs are tired.

I'm a shaggy dog.

Doghouse

The other day
My mom told Dad,
"You're in the doghouse."
And she sounded mad.

Why was she mad
That he is in my house?
She lives here too.
She's not with a mouse.
Maybe she just wishes,
As I do, that Dad
Would be home more often.
Then neither of us would be mad.

Tired Dogs

One day after cleaning
And cooking all day,
My mom told her friend,
"My dogs are tired."
Now what did she mean?
First of all,
She has but one dog,
And that is me.
At least, she better not
Have any more,
Or I'll be very sad.
Anyway, I wasn't tired.
So how can she say,
"My dogs are tired?"
Who can tell me
What silly Mom means?

Shaggy Dog

I heard her on the phone:
"I'm a shaggy dog."
She's no more like me
Than a bird or hog.
I don't want her
To be like me;
She'd not be a good dog
With two legs and feet.
She can't run or growl
Or give the love I can.
And she moves around
Too much, and
I love her the way she is:
A little bit crazy,
But she is my mom,
Even though a bit hazy
On what she means
With her silly speech.
At least she doesn't
Talk too long or preach.

The Beauty Shop

Hooray, hooray, hooray!
I went to the beauty
shop today.
(I've heard a rumor
that I should say groomer,
but everyone knows
that's where Mom goes.)
And once again,
I am bright
and clean and look
just right.
Hooray, hooray, hooray
for the beauty shop today.

Smarts

My mom was asked
The other day
If I was smart.
This is what she had to say:

"Yes, my dog is smart,
But perhaps not the way
You are thinking of
On this bright, sunny day.
My dog does not
Subtract or add,
And she is usually great,
But sometimes, she is bad."

Hey, Mom, watch it—
You have just made me sad.

"My dog's smarts
Come in a form
Far and above
The *usual* norm.
When I talk,
She tilts her head just so,
Her loving way
Of letting me know
She cares very much
About what I say.
This is always true
On any and every day.

"Her sensitivity shows,
As does her constant love;
No matter my mood,
She's a peaceful dove.
And she writes poetry
Extremely well,
Verse which is always
Clear as a bell."

Now, Mom, you've got it;
What you've said is swell.

"So is my dog smart?
Yes, exceptionally smart.
She has me 'round her finger
And reigns high in my heart."

I'm a Senior

I sleep a whole lot
a good part of the day.
And oh, my aching knees:
I think you know
about such things
if you are older too.
Young things can't imagine
this could ever be true.
They'll never let this
happen to them,
they proclaim.
Ha! Wish I could be
around to see them when
they're past sixty-three!

Ice

I went out
first thing to
potty,
but my paws
went this way and that,
and then
splat.
my body hit the ground.
Why?

(An inch of ice was everywhere. Many two-leggers broke bones
with falls, but I didn't, and neither did Mom or Dad.)

Grandma

Mom said she died.
Mom and Dad
Sat and cried.

I love them lots,
And I tried my best
To help them out,
But I confessed

To them that I
Also felt sad,
For being with her
Had made me glad.

She scratched my head,
Called me "little one,"
Slipped me treats,
More than a crumb.

I seemed to always
Bring her delight,
And she always looked
A beauty in my sight.

I miss you, Grandma;
I'm glad you were mine
And that now you abide
With God, the divine.

I Love My Folks

I hug my mom and
Kiss my dad,
And I rejoice
For I'm so glad

That I own them.
This is true;
You've read my book
And know all I do.

It is now time
To leave Mom's lap.
No more work—
I'm going to nap.

AFTERWORD

Rivé lived both a longer and shorter time than she should have. An acquaintance just had to have his eighteen–year-old Bichon Frise put down. Sixteen to eighteen years is how long I would expect a small dog to live.

But I had known for at least four years that Rivé wouldn't live that long. When we had to have her put to sleep, her doctor said, "She has lived longer than I thought she would."

Five years ago Rivé became very weak. She quit eating. Our veterinarian sent her to an internal medicine vet who determined she had some form of inflammatory bowel disease. The treatment was prednisone, but being on prednisone for years had a negative effect on her kidneys. She was able to do well with a half a prednisone tablet every other day. On the other days we gave her a half tablet of azathioprine.

We had just gotten her bowel problem under control when her skin broke out. She needed to see a dermatologist. The diagnosis was pemphigus, which can go into remission, as hers did, or grow worse. The prednisone was the treatment for this condition.

Within the past year, urinary tract infections occurred more frequently. The vet prescribed shots to be given to her seven continuous days at the beginning of every month. This prevented the infections.

But her body wore out. Her system shut down. She dropped to fourteen pounds from nineteen pounds in a couple of weeks, and then she lost three more pounds before she died.

My mother quit eating before her death. Rivé did the same thing.

She wrote one last poem the morning of the day we took her in to be put to sleep.

Love and Trust

I trust you, Mom,
and I love you.
I know you know
the right thing to do.

I don't want to leave,
so I won't say, "good-bye."
But I will say "so long,
I'll see you in the by-and-by."

I'll be in touch
with you from heaven;
being your dog
was like living in heaven.

I trust you, Mom.
You're doing what is right,
and very soon now,
I'll walk in light.